PIANO
SOLOS
HORIZON
SERIES

*Includes Playing Tips
& Lyric Section*

**ARRANGED BY**
**PHILLIP**
**KEVEREN**

INTERMEDIATE
# THE BEST OF
# THE BEATLES
## VOLUME 1
### FEATURING HEY JUDE & YESTERDAY

THE HORIZON SERIES picks up where **MORE FOR YOUR METHOD** leaves off, featuring authentic sounding arrangements for the intermediate-level pianist. Avoiding the melody-plus-chords approach used in most pop collections, these easy piano solos feature a fully developed left-hand part designed to make any player sound like a pro! In addition, you will find a special lyric section PLUS… "lessons" to guide you through the more difficult parts of each song.

HAL•LEONARD™
CORPORATION
7777 W. BLUEMOUND RD. P.O. BOX 13819 MILWAUKEE, WI 53213

T0051133

ISBN 0-7935-1474-6

PIANO SOLOS
*HORIZON SERIES*

INTERMEDIATE

# THE BEST OF
# THE BEATLES
# VOLUME 1

# LYRICS

## A DAY IN THE LIFE

Words and Music by JOHN LENNON and PAUL McCARTNEY

I read the news today oh boy
About a lucky man who made the grade
And though the news was rather sad
Well I just had to laugh
I saw the photograph
He blew his mind out in a car
He didn't notice that the lights had changed
A crowd of people stood and stared
They'd seen his face before
Nobody was really sure
If he was from the House of Lords.
I saw a film today oh boy
The English Army had just won the war
A crowd of people turned away
But I just had to look
Having read the book.
I'd love to turn you on
Woke up, got out of bed,
Dragged a comb across my head
Found my way downstairs and drank a cup,
And looking up I noticed I was late.
Found my coat and grabbed my hat
Made the bus in seconds flat
Found my way upstairs and had a smoke,
And somebody spoke and I went into a dream
I heard the news today oh boy
Four thousand holes in Blackburn, Lancashire
And though the holes were rather small
They had to count them all
Now they know how many holes it takes
To fill the Albert Hall.
I'd love to turn you on.

## HERE COMES THE SUN

By GEORGE HARRISON

Here comes the sun, here comes the sun,
And I say it's all right.
Little darling it's been a long cold lonely winter,
Little darling it feels like years since it's been here.
Here comes the sun, here comes the sun,
And I say it's all right.
Little darling the smiles returning to their faces,
Little darling it seems like years since it's been here,
Here comes the sun, here comes the sun,
And I say it's all right.
Sun, sun, sun, here it comes.
Sun, sun, sun, here it comes.
Sun, sun, sun, here it comes.
Sun, sun, sun, here it comes.
Little darling I feel that ice is slowly melting,
Little darling it seems like years since it's been clear,
Here comes the sun, here comes the sun,
It's all right, it's all right.

## THE FOOL ON THE HILL

Words and Music by JOHN LENNON and PAUL McCARTNEY

Day after day, alone on a hill,
The man with the foolish grin is keeping perfectly still
But nobody wants to know him,
They can see that he's just a fool
And he never gives an answer.
But the fool on the hill sees the sun going down
And the eyes in his head see the world spinning round.
Well on the way, head in a cloud,
The man of a thousand voices talking perfectly loud.
But nobody ever hears him
Or the sound he appears to make
And he never seems to notice.
But the fool on the hill sees the sun going down
And the eyes in his head see the world spinning round.
And nobody seems to like him,
They can tell what he wants to do
And he never shows his feelings.
But the fool on the hill sees the sun going down
And the eyes in his head see the world spinning round.
He never listens to them,
He knows that they're the fools.
They don't like him.
The fool on the hill sees the sun going down
And the eyes in his head see the world spinning round.

## HERE, THERE AND EVERYWHERE

Words and Music by JOHN LENNON and PAUL McCARTNEY

To lead a better life, I need my love to be here.
Here, making each day of the year,
Changing my life with a wave of her hand.
Nobody can deny that there's something there.
There, running my hands through her hair,
Both of us thinking how good it can be.
Someone is speaking but she doesn't know he's there.
I want her ev'rywhere, and if she's beside me I know I need never care,
But to love her is to meet her ev'rywhere,
Knowing that love is to share,
Each one believing that love never dies,
Watching her eyes and hoping I'm always there.
I want her ev'rywhere, and if she's beside me I know I need never care,
But to love her is to meet her ev'rywhere,
Knowing that love is to share,
Each one believing that love never dies,
Watching her eyes and hoping I'm always there.
To be there and ev'rywhere,
Here, there and ev'rywhere.

# HEY JUDE

Words and Music by JOHN LENNON and PAUL McCARTNEY

Hey Jude don't make it bad,
Take a sad song and make it better,
Remember, to let her into your heart,
Then you can start to make it better.
Hey Jude don't be afraid,
You were made to go out and get her,
The minute you let her under your skin,
Then you begin to make it better.
And anytime you feel the pain,
Hey Jude refrain,
Don't carry the world upon your shoulders.
For well you know that it's a fool,
Who plays it cool
By making his world a little colder.
Hey Jude don't let me down,
You have found her now go and get her,
Remember (Hey Jude) to let her into your hear,
Then you can start to make it better.
So let it out and let it in
Hey Jude begin,
You're waiting for someone to perform with.
And don't you know that it's just you.
Hey Jude, you'll do,
The movement you need is on your shoulder.
Hey Jude, don't make it bad,
Take a sad song and make it better,
Remember to let her under your skin,
Then you'll begin to make it better.

# IN MY LIFE

Words and Music by JOHN LENNON and PAUL McCARTNEY

There are places I'll remember
All my life, though some have changed,
Some forever, not for better,
Some have gone and some remain.
All these places had their moments,
With lovers and friends I still can recall,
Some are dead and some are living,
In my life I've loved them all.
But of all these friends and lovers,
There is no one compared with you,
And these mem'ries lose their meaning
When I think of love as something new.
Though I know I'll never lose affection
For people and things that went before,
I know I'll often stop and think about them,
In my life I'll love you more.
Though I know I'll never lose affection
For people and things that went before,
I know I'll often stop and think about them
In my life I'll love you more.
In my life I'll love you more.

# NORWEGIAN WOOD (THIS BIRD HAS FLOWN)

Words and Music by JOHN LENNON and PAUL McCARTNEY

I once had a girl,
Or I should say
She once had me.
She showed me her room,
Isn't it good?
Norwegian wood.
She asked me to stay and she told me to sit anywhere,
So I looked around and I noticed there wasn't a chair.
I sat on a rug
Biding my time,
Drinking her wine.
We talked until two,
And then she said,
'It's time for bed.'
She told me she worked in the morning and started to laugh,
I told her I didn't, and crawled off to sleep in the bath.
And when I awoke
I was alone,
This bird had flown,
So I lit a fire,
Isn't it good?
Norwegian wood.

# SOMETHING

By GEORGE HARRISON

Something in the way she moves
Attracts me like no other lover,
Something in the way she woos me.
I don't want to leave her now,
You know I believe and how.
Somewhere in her smile she knows
That I don't need no other lover.
Something in her style that shows me.
I don't want to leave her now,
You know I believe and how.
You're asking me will my love grow,
I don't know, I don't know.
You stick around now it may show,
I don't know, I don't know.
Something in the way she knows
And all I have to do is think of her,
Something in the things she shows me.
I don't want to leave her now,
You know I believe and how.

# WHILE MY GUITAR GENTLY WEEPS

By GEORGE HARRISON

look at you all see the love there that's sleeping
While my guitar gently weeps.
I look at the floor and I see it needs sweeping
Still my guitar gently weeps.
I don't know why nobody told you
How to unfold your love,
I don't know how someone controlled you
They bought and sold you.
I look at the world and I notice it's turning
While my guitar gently weeps.
With every mistake we must surely be learning,
Still my guitar gently weeps.
I don't know how you were diverted
You were perverted too.
I don't know how you were inverted
No-one alerted you.
I look at you all see the love there that's sleeping,
While my guitar gently weeps.
I then look at you all,
Still my guitar gently weeps.

# YESTERDAY

Words and Music by JOHN LENNON and PAUL McCARTNEY

Yesterday, all my troubles seemed so far away,
Now it looks as though they're here to stay,
Oh I believe in yesterday.
Suddenly, I'm not half the man I used to be,
There's a shadow hanging over me,
Oh yesterday came suddenly...
Why she had to go I don't know. She wouldn't say.
I said something wrong, now I long for yesterday,
Yesterday, Love was such an easy game to play,
Now I need a place to hide away,
Oh I believe in yesterday...

# LESSON: A DAY IN THE LIFE

This arrangement introduces three separate sections: the verse, the bridge, and the restatement of the verse. Each has moments of contrast within itself, but the real contrast occurs *between* the three major sections.

The verse needs a smooth, legato attitude; play the melody (tossed about between the two hands) gracefully and lyrically. The bridge, starting at the bottom of the second page, needs a bouncy detached feeling. Emphasize the eighth-note pulse by playing the left hand detached. The end of the bridge gets frantic, so when the verse comes back in on page four, make sure you again play the melody smoothly, as if you are singing the melody through the piano.

To coordinate the opening rhythm, step back from the piano and tap out the following exercise on your knees. Use a metronome, if you have one, to help you keep the tempo steady. The upstem notes are for the right hand, while the downstem notes are for the left.

Now put these two parts together, making sure that the sixteenth note figure lines up with the steady eighth-note pulse of the right hand.

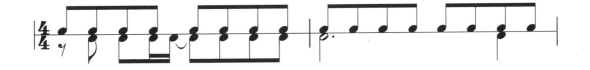

Now tap the next figure. How does this compare with the first figure?

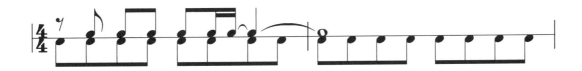

Put these two figures together and tap the next example.

Now try playing the second line of the first page. You have already worked out the rhythmic coordination between the two hands. Simply add the pitches.

# A DAY IN THE LIFE

Words and Music by
JOHN LENNON and PAUL McCARTNEY

**Slowly**

*detached*

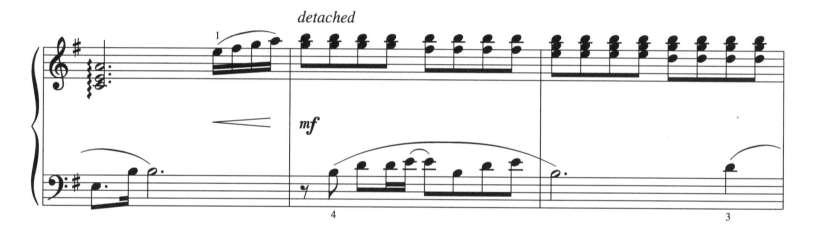

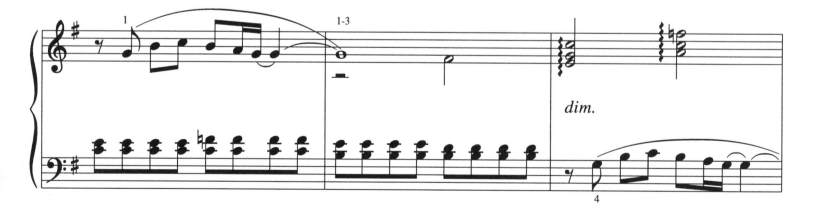

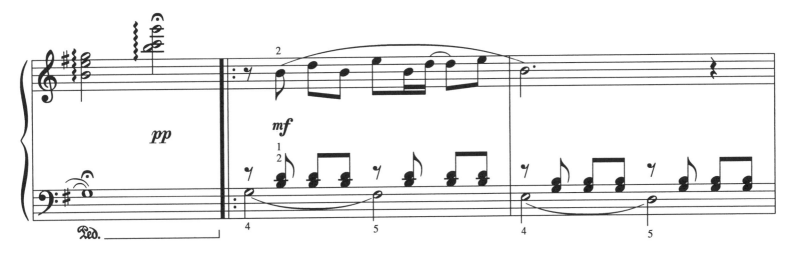

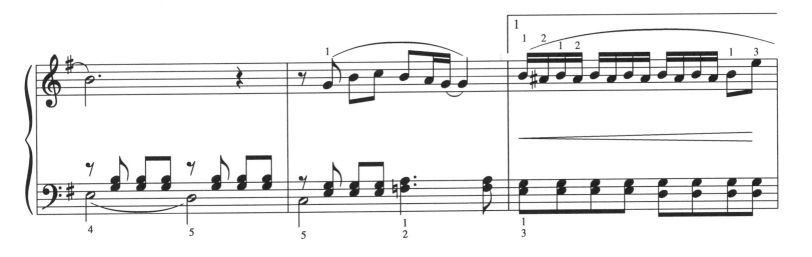

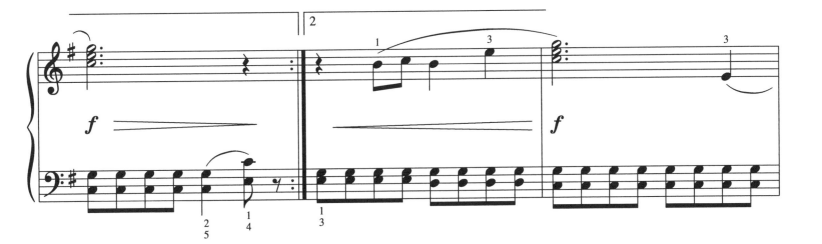

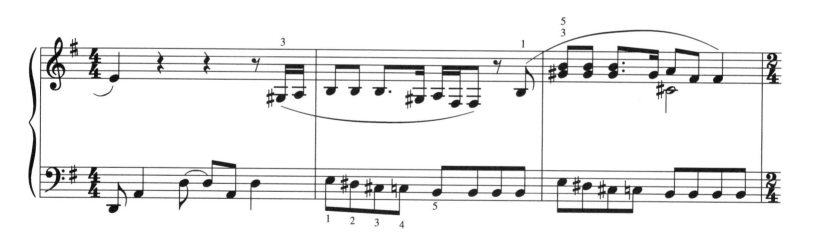

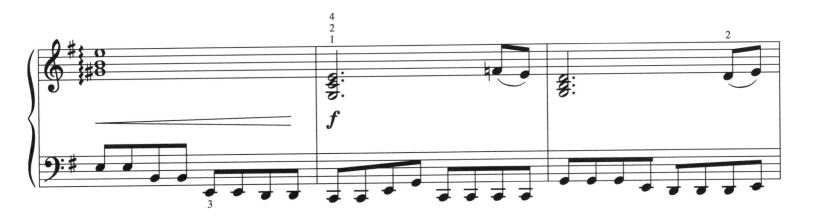

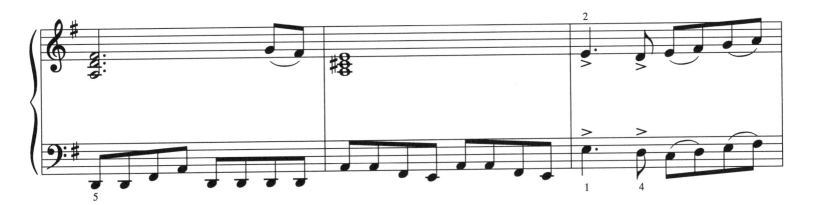

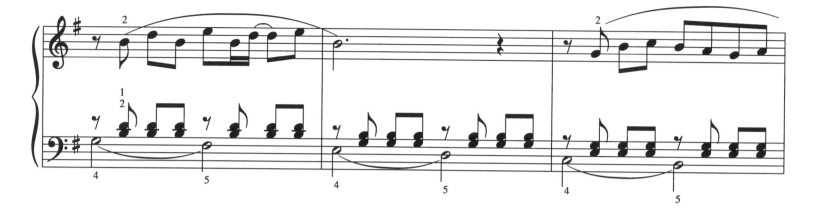

# LESSON: THE FOOL ON THE HILL

This song needs a strong two-beat feeling, one that sways back and forth with beats one and three. Imagine walking in time to the music, with your feet landing on beats one and three. Put a lot of weight on each foot.

Practice the important skill of getting from one hand position to another as smoothly as possible, by going back and forth between the chords in the examples below. Using your left hand, move from the first to the second chord as quickly and cleanly as you can.

Now take a look at the bottom of the first page. Even though the left hand is arpeggiated, the notes are the same and the hand position is identical. The same can be said about the left-hand figure in the second line of the third page. By "blocking out" arpeggios and practicing the hand position shifts, your fingers will know where to go as a group.

To help with the coordination between the hands on the second page, try the example below. Tap on your knees, tapping the upstem notes with your right hand and the downstem notes with your left hand.

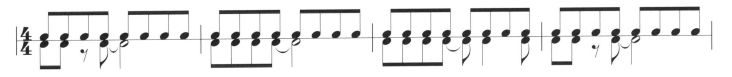

Now play the passage as it appears in the music shown below. By isolating the rhythm first, the hands will already know what to do.

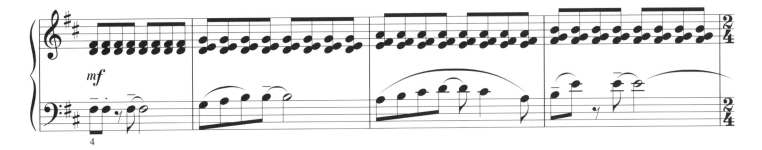

# THE FOOL ON THE HILL

Words and Music by
JOHN LENNON and PAUL McCARTNEY

**Slowly, very expressively**

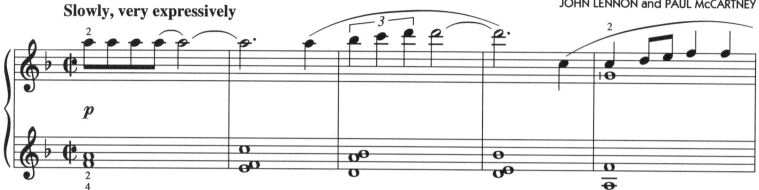

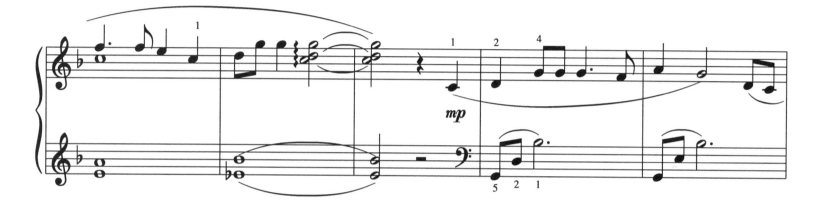

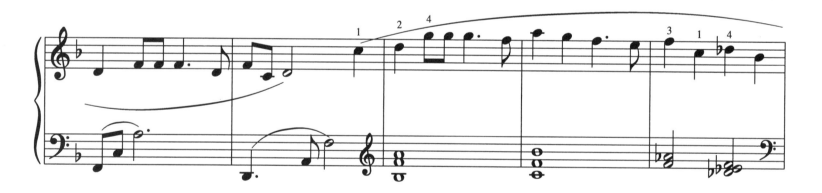

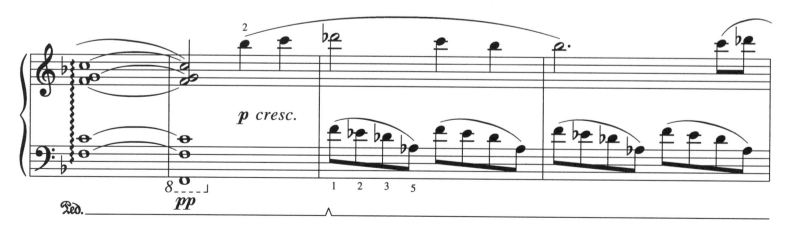

**MCA** music publishing

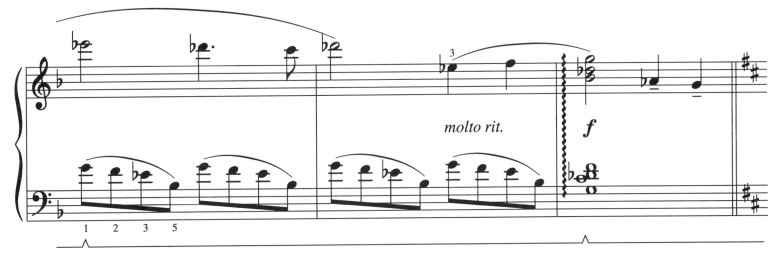

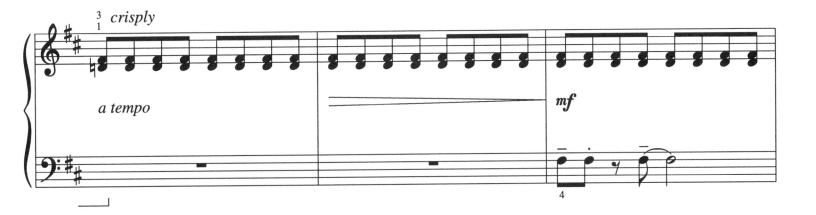

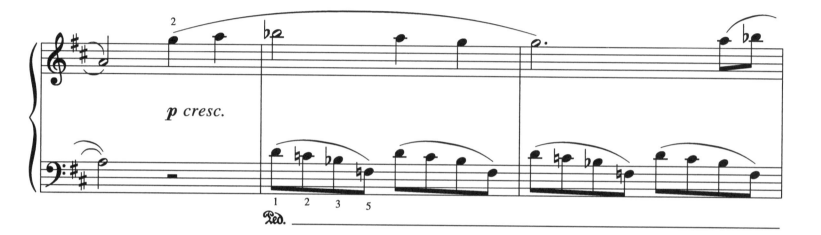

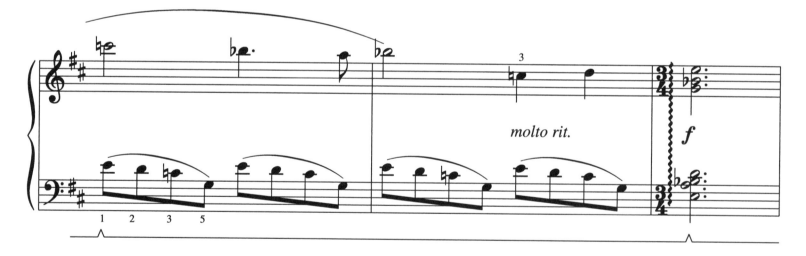

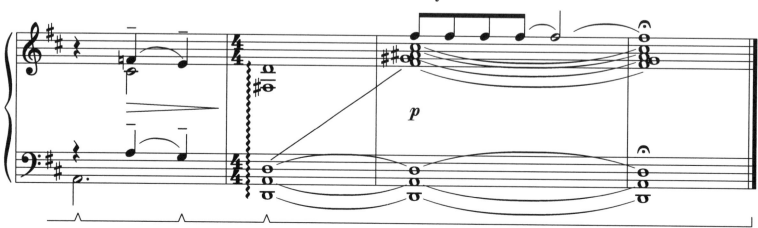

# LESSON: HERE COMES THE SUN

This song features an interesting rhythmic figure that could, on first glance, strike panic into all but the least faint of heart. Yet upon closer inspection and with a little explanation, this rhythm loses its mystery. Subdivide the beat and your panic will disappear.

In 4/4 time, eighth notes usually occur in groups of four, which divide the measure into two equal parts. (To impress your friends, talk about the "agogic accents" of this grouping.)

Nothing necessarily keeps us from clumping eighth notes into other groupings. Let's take a look at what happens when they appear in threes instead.

Yet the measure is not in two equal parts anymore. It takes a measure and a half to get to the start of the pattern and three full measures until the pattern begins beat one again.

Take a look at the top of the second page and see how the eighth notes are grouped together. (Even the phrase marks are giving a hint!) Four groups of three are followed by a group of four, so the pattern comes out evenly by the first beat of the next measure. Make sure the eighth note doesn't change tempo. Its time value is the same; only the accents are shifted to groups of three. Notice how the left hand punctuates this rhythm with the dotted quarter notes.

# HERE COMES THE SUN

By GEORGE HARRISON

**Cheerfully**

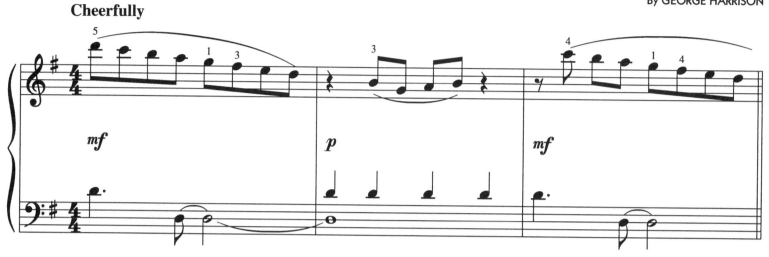

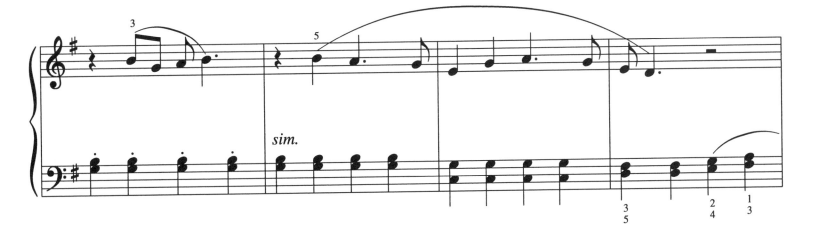

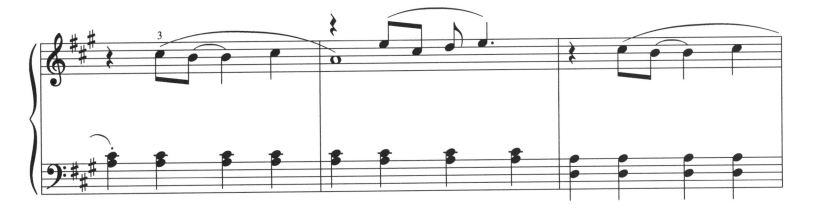

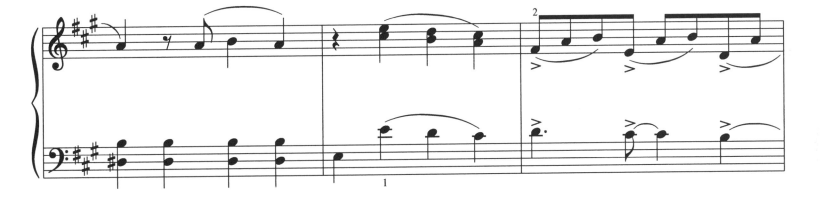

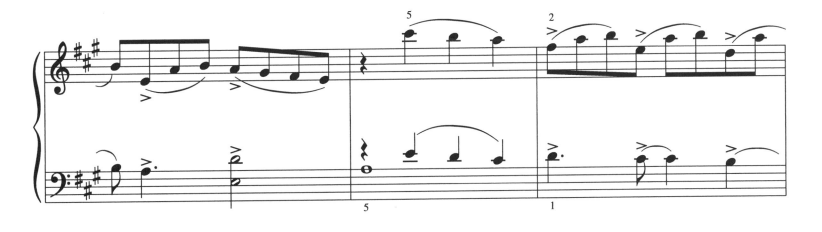

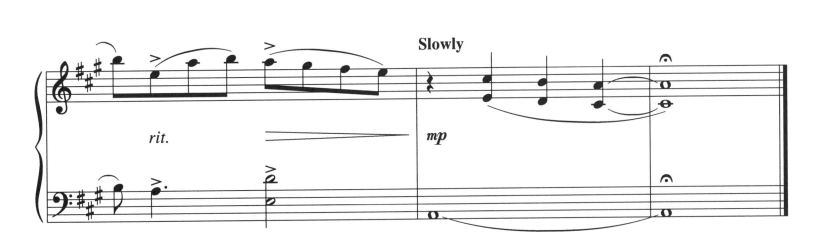

# LESSON: HERE, THERE AND EVERYWHERE

This arrangement feaures wonderfully simple harmony that is nevertheless effective. Let's take a closer look at some of it.

This song is in the key of G major (one sharp in the key signature). Below is the G major scale.

Let's build triads (3 note chords) on each scale tone. These triads are called *diatonic triads* because all the notes are *diatonic* to our key. (Diatonic is a fancy way of saying "in the key.") The triad built on the G, or first scale degree, is called a "one" chord. A triad built on the second scale degree, A, is called a "two" chord, and so on up the scale.

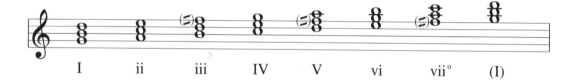

Let's look at the left-hand part in measures four and five. Stack up all the notes that occur in beats one and two and beats three and four. (The left hand is playing arpeggios or broken chords.)

Compare the diatonic triads listed earlier to the chords found in measures four and five. Even though the notes are an octave lower, the chord content is the same. Measure four starts with a "one" chord and then goes to a "two" chord. Measure five continues this chord *progression* by going to a "three" chord followed by a "four" chord. This chord progression is called a diatonic chord progression because all the chords used in it are diatonic, or in the key (in our case the key of G major).

# HERE, THERE AND EVERYWHERE

Words and Music by
JOHN LENNON and PAUL McCARTNEY

**Slowly, freely**

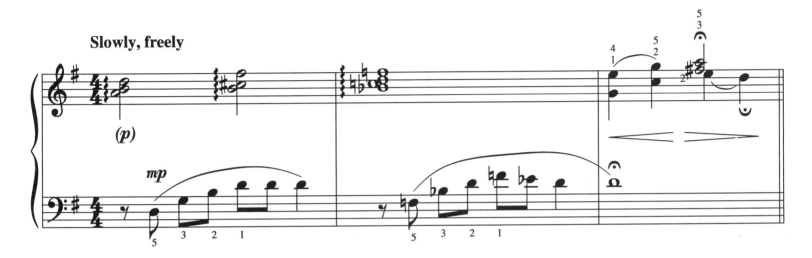

**Moderately and expressively**

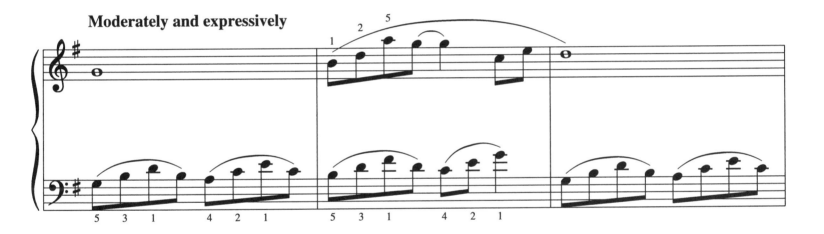

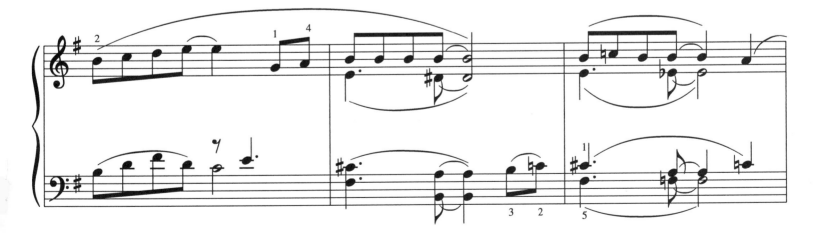

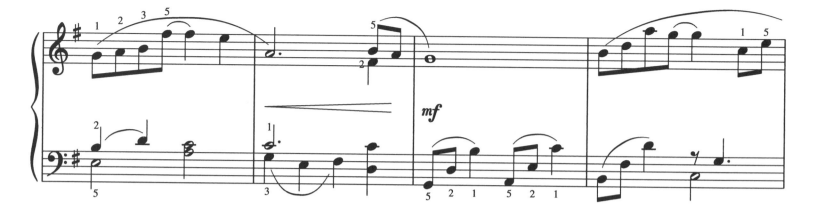

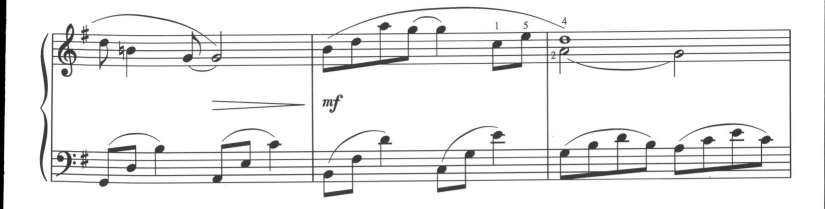

# LESSON: HEY JUDE

This song contains one of the most famous sections in pop music: the "outroduction," "da, da da, da-da-da-da... Hey Jude" part at the end. This segment repeats three times. To make it effective in a solo piano setting, build in intensity each time. Keep the crescendo increasing, but not too quickly, or you'll run out of room to grow dynamically. After all, the first dynamic marking is forte, so little room exists to build volume. Each time the phrase repeats itself, make it more accented by emphasizing the eighth-note pulse. This effect will drive the music forward, making the ending more exciting.

The melody gets tossed between the hands throughout this arrangement. Keep the continuity going through all this hand switching by keeping the melody prominent.

The eighth note creates the underlying pulse of this entire song. This eighth-note "buzz" will make even the longer notes (half- and whole-notes) seem to move forward.

If you keep the feel of the underlying eighth-note pulse in your body, your playing will have more direction and drive.

# HEY JUDE

Words and Music by
JOHN LENNON and PAUL McCARTNEY

**Slowly**

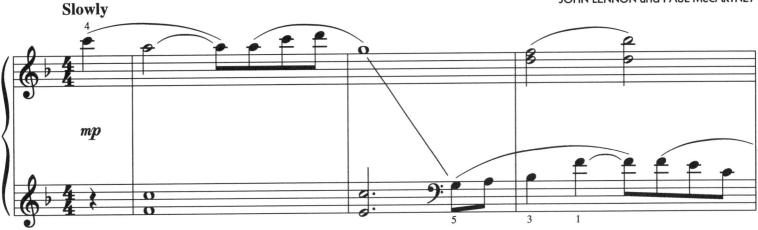

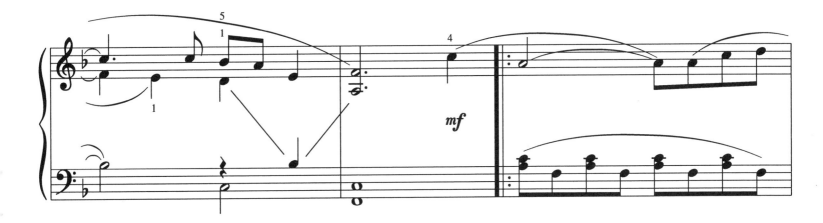

MCA music publishing

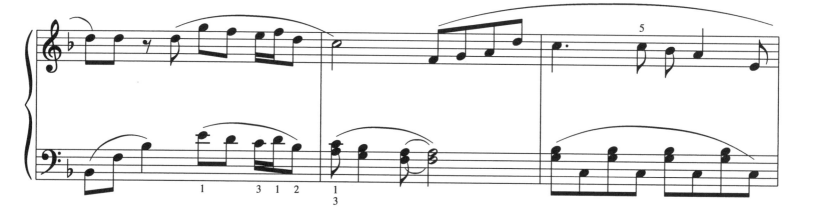

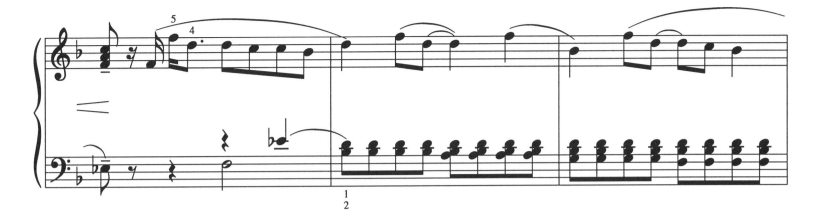

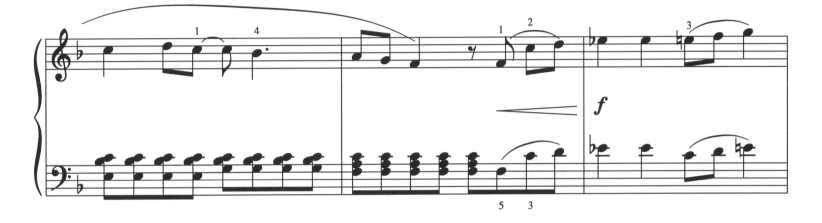

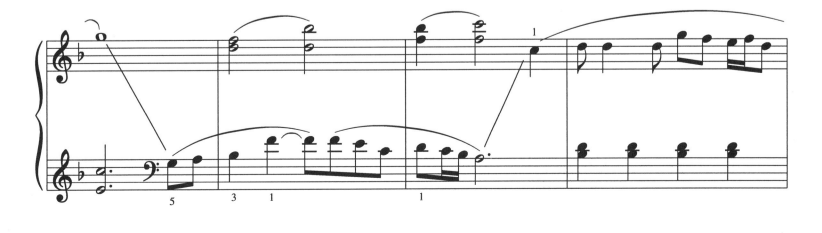

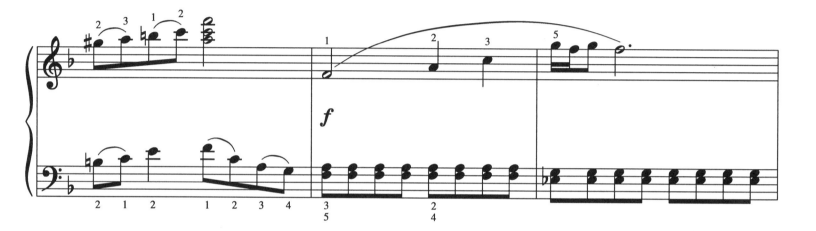

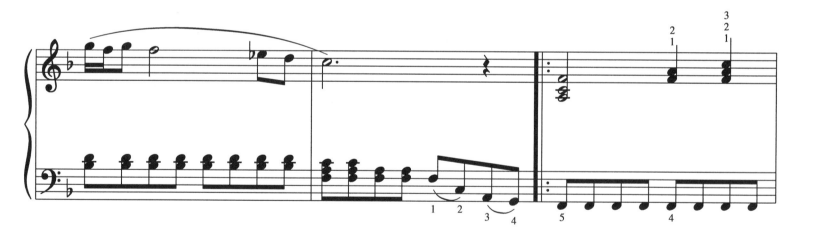

# LESSON: IN MY LIFE

This song features a short instrumental section reminiscent of the Baroque period. This musical era ran from about 1600 to 1750 and included such famous composers as Vivaldi, Handel and J.S. Bach. The Beatles imitated Baroque style in this song, both in the instrumentation they selected and in their choice of notes and rhythms.

This "Baroque" section begins at the top of the third page, with the second ending. The left hand plays a broken chord accompaniment (called an Alberti bass) typically found in works of this period. An effective practice method for a pattern such as this is to "unbreak" the chord. By blocking out the hand positions, your hand will have a much clearer outline to follow than just going by a note-by-note plan.

Play the line below with your left hand moving from one hand position to the next smoothly. Don't be in a hurry. Your hand needs time to learn the positions.

Play the figure below with your left hand. After practicing the "blocked" chords, your hand should be able to shift to each position in a way that makes you feel like all the notes are "under the fingers."

Now put the right hand with the left. Play the right hand while you play the left hand in blocked position before playing both hands together as written. By tackling only one difficulty at a time, practicing can be a more productive and enjoyable time.

# IN MY LIFE

Words and Music by
JOHN LENNON and PAUL McCARTNEY

MCA music publishing

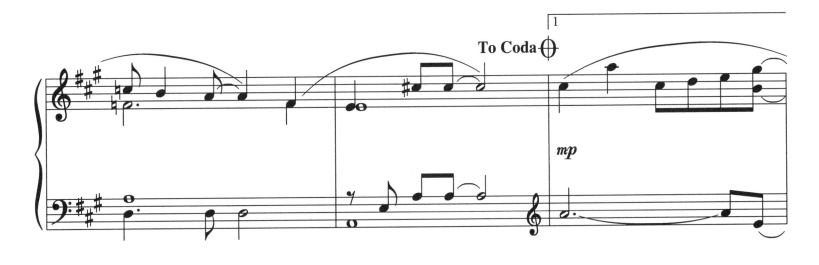

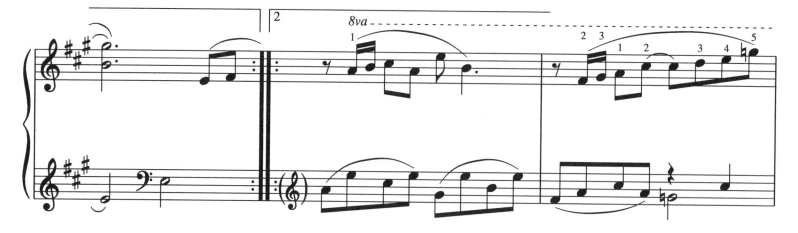

**D.S. al Coda**

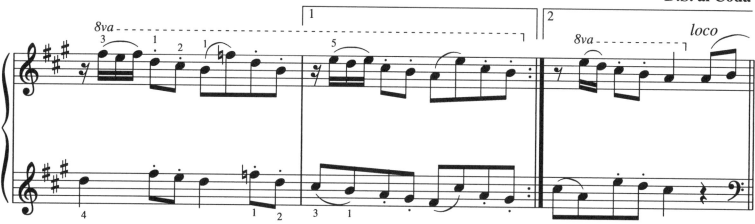

**CODA**

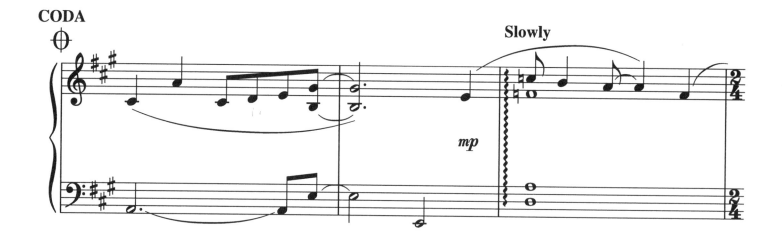

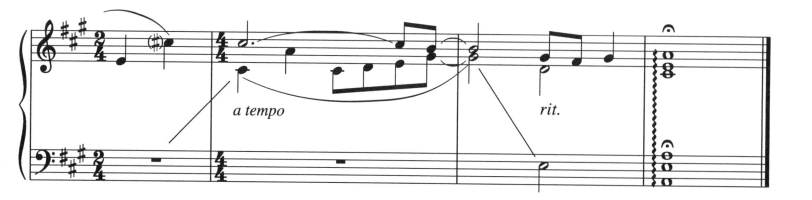

# LESSON: NORWEGIAN WOOD (THIS BIRD HAS FLOWN)

This arrangement appears in a two-part form. The first section (A) presents the melody played in the left hand with a persistently repeating (*ostinato*) eighth-note figure in the right hand. This right-hand figure repeats until the second line of page two, so it certainly qualifies as an ostinato!

The second part, or "B" section, finds the melody moved to the right hand. It occurs mostly in single notes with some countermelodies for spice. These countermelodies (this technique is known as *counterpoint*) are usually added where the movement of the melody stops. For instance, at the end of the first line on the third page the melody is a long held note (high C). Instead of simply holding the melody note while the left hand plays merrily away, a "counterline" is added to keep the motion moving forward. Most pop music uses this technique when writing background vocals.

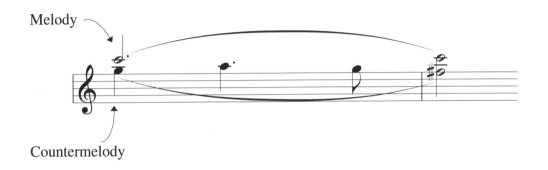

Another countermelody can be found at the bottom of the third page. In measures one and three, the melody uses a dotted half note, while the counterline keeps the motion moving forward with the eighth-note/half-note figure.

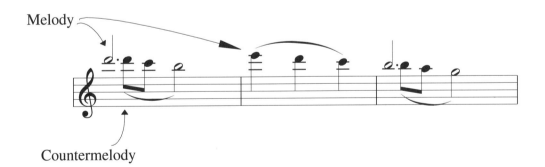

Yet, both the melody and the countermelody share the same first note. Let your wrist drop into the figure, accenting the melody note (also the first note of the countermelody) and playing the counterline as your wrist moves back up.

# NORWEGIAN WOOD
## (THIS BIRD HAS FLOWN)

Words and Music by
JOHN LENNON and PAUL McCARTNEY

Moderately, in 1 ( ♩. = 45 )

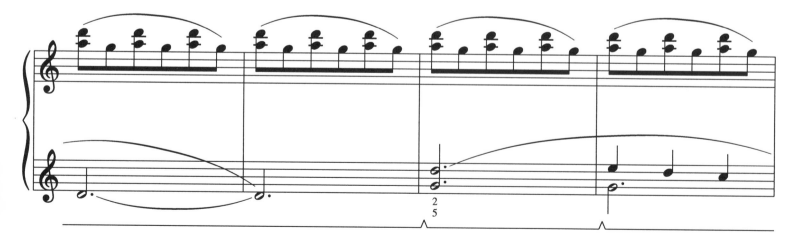

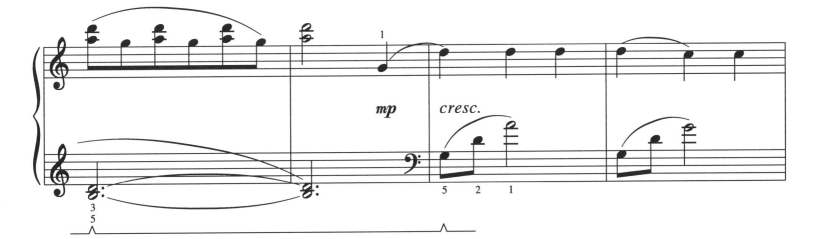

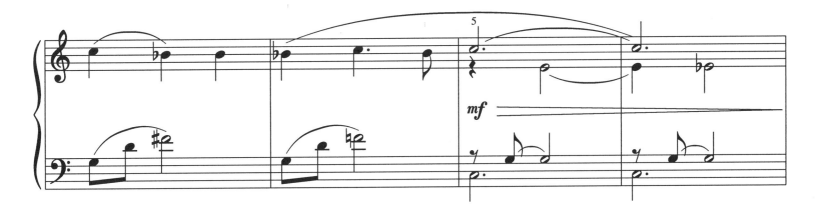

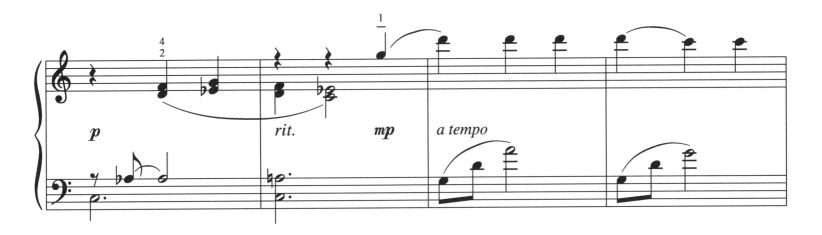

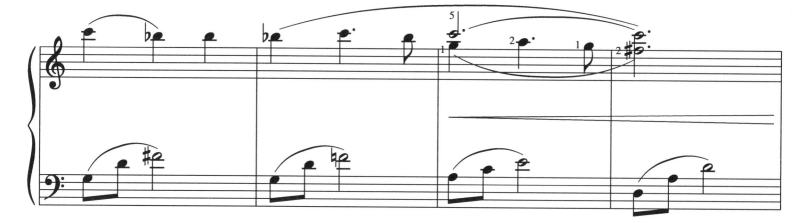

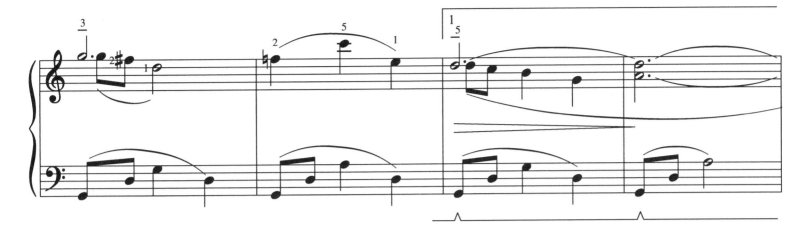

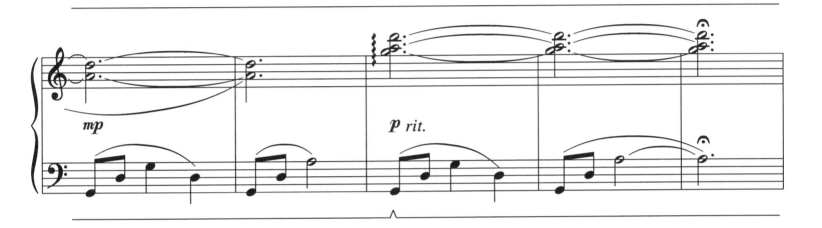

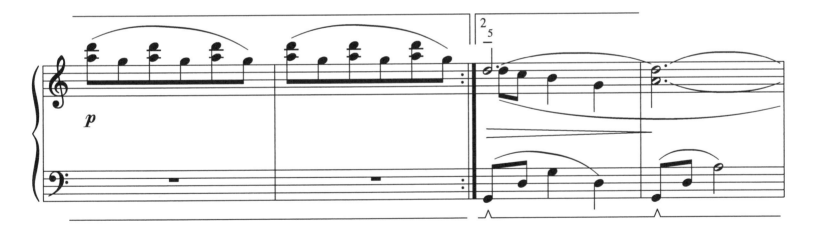

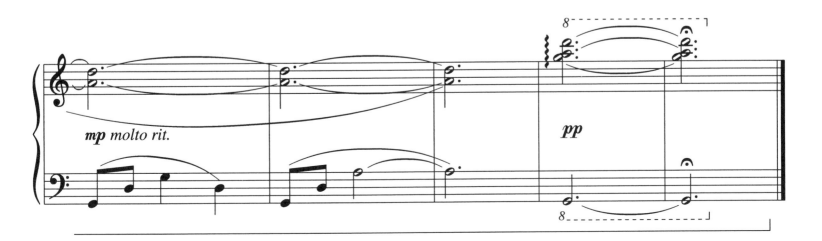

# LESSON: SOMETHING

This arrangement uses an A-A-B-A form, the "A" being the verse and the "B" being the bridge. This in itself isn't particularly earth-shattering until we look at the harmonic relationship between the verse and the chorus. The verse appears in our familiar key of C major, but the bridge makes the seemingly out-in-left-field jump to the key of A major.

While the jump into the bridge, and into A major is a surprise, the two keys are not all that distant from one another. Let's take a look at how the bridge winds its way back into the key of C to find out how these two keys are related.

One of the most basic chord movements, or progressions, is root movement by a perfect fifth. This movement gives us the familiar dominant-tonic relationship, or I to V. For instance, a major chord built on the note G followed by a major chord built on the note C has a dominant-tonic relationship. Let's take that structure a little farther and see where we end up.

Start at the note C and go up consecutive perfect fifths and see what happens. From C we go up a fifth to the note G. For our purposes here, the chord quality (major, minor, whatever...) is less important than the chord's root. Going up another fifth from G gets us to the note D. The following chart continues this upward movement.

C-G-D-A-E-B

Take a look at the example below and follow the chord movement. The chords start at A major and follow our progression of fifths until we are back in our home key of C major.

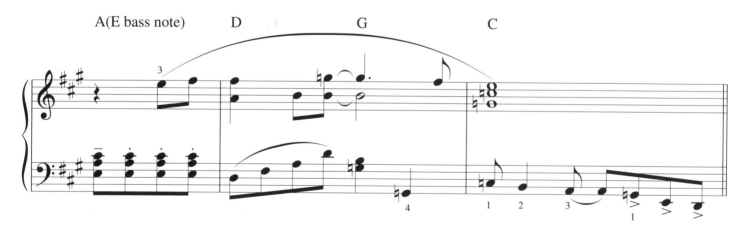

# SOMETHING

By GEORGE HARRISON

**Slowly**

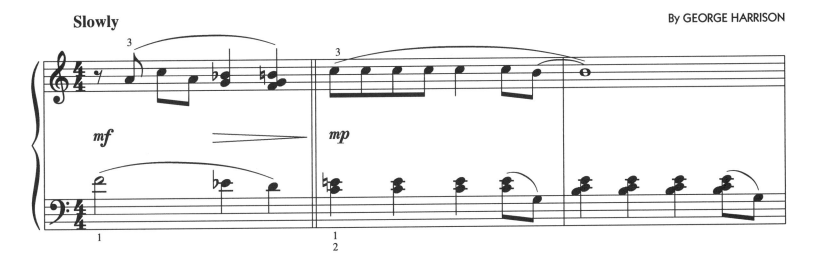

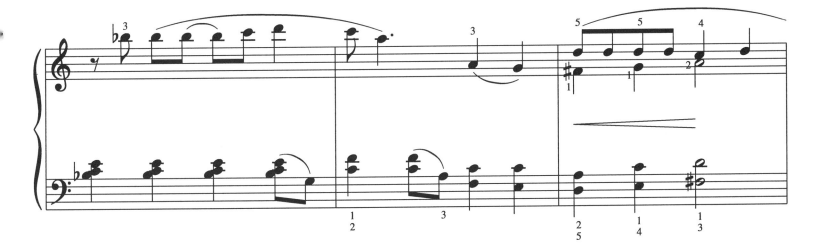

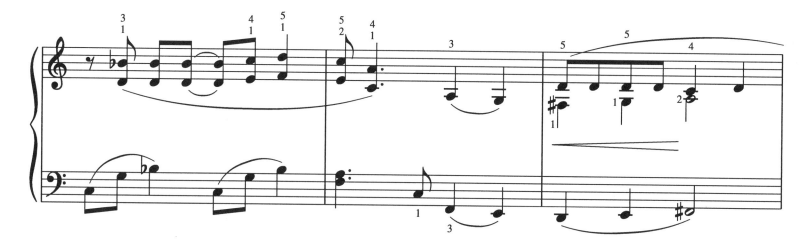

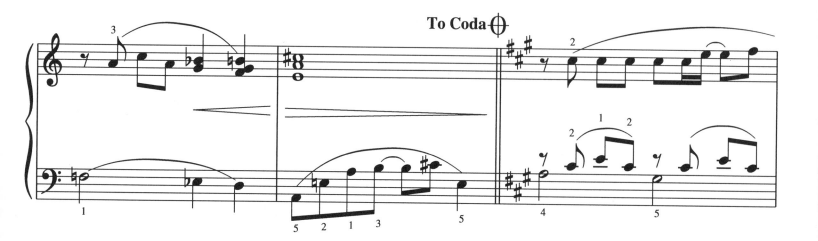

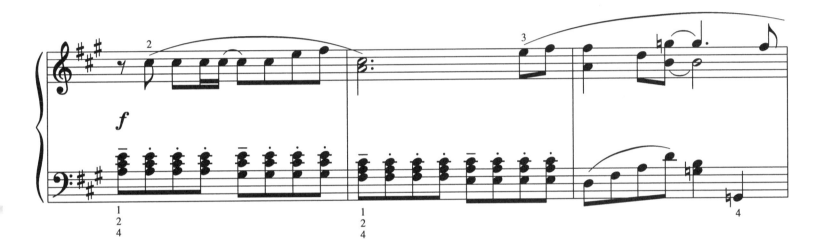

**D.S. al Coda**

**CODA**

*rit.*

# LESSON: WHILE MY GUITAR GENTLY WEEPS

While the title suggests this is a tender, melancholy song, the original Beatles recording presents a driving, raw, rock-and-roll sound. Apparently the guitar isn't weeping in sadness, but in upset and anger. Take an agressive posture with the music, giving your interpretation an angry edge.

Contrast this agitated feeling with a smoother, more refined texture in the opening verse. The verse, starting at the sign on the second line, is in four-bar phrases. Each phrase alternates angry-calm. The left-hand accompaniment style is the tip-off. Treat the quarter notes in the first four bars with a *secco* (dry without pedal) effect. Use finger legato in the right hand so the left hand can sound detached.

Play the second four bars with the pedal to create a more resonant timbre. Set this contrast up even more by creating a softer dynamic level.

The next four bars are without pedal again. Watch the fingering for the double thirds. Although using the pedal would make an easier fingering possible, don't give in. The pedal will smear the left-hand quarter notes together, taking away that agressive edge.

The bridge, starting at the double bar features a smooth eighth-note accompaniment pattern. Let's break it down into its hand positions before tackling the whole thing.

Play the following line, using the exact written fingering.

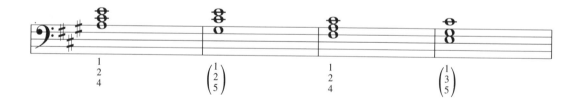

Now play the line as written in the music. The hand shifts should feel smooth and easy. If they don't, go back to the "blocked" hand positions and practice the shifts some more. Use this technique of blocking out hand positions wherever the hand jumps from position to position.

# WHILE MY GUITAR GENTLY WEEPS

By GEORGE HARRISON

**Moderately**

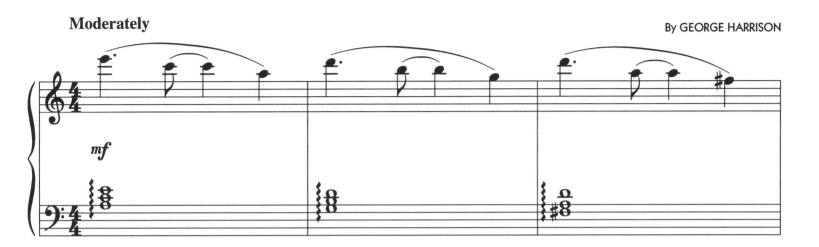

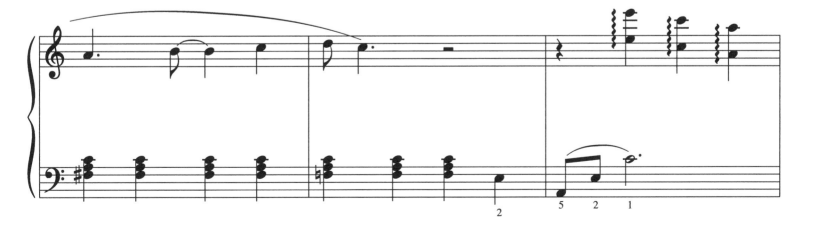

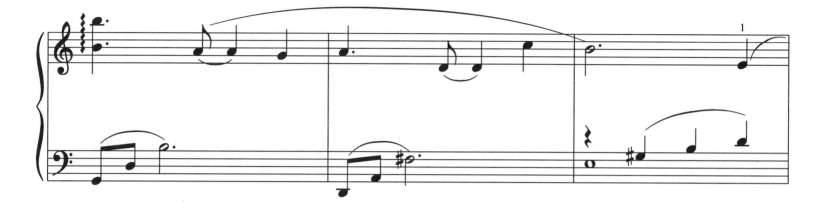

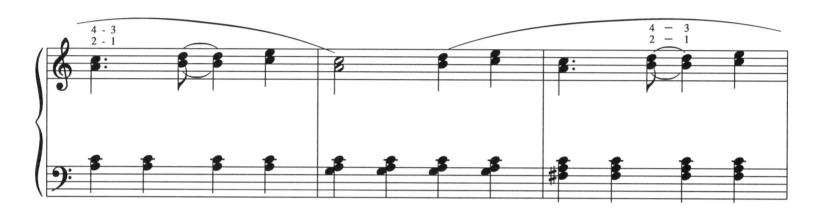

**To Coda** ⊕

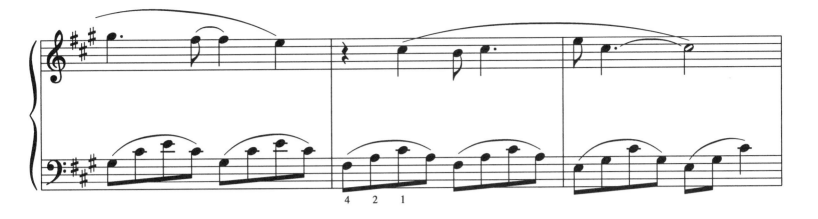

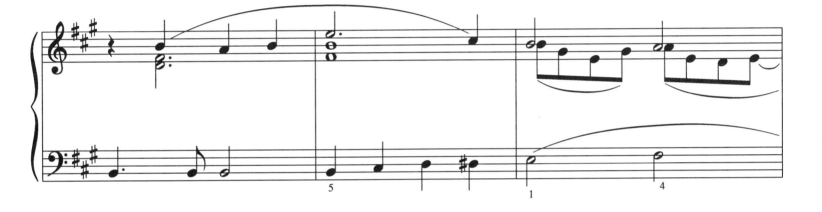

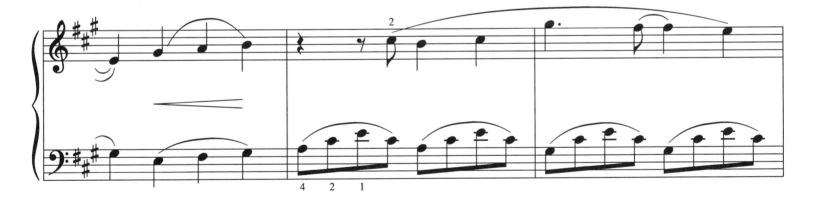

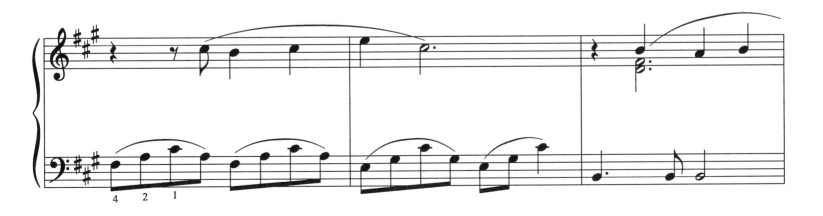

**D.S. al Coda**

**CODA**

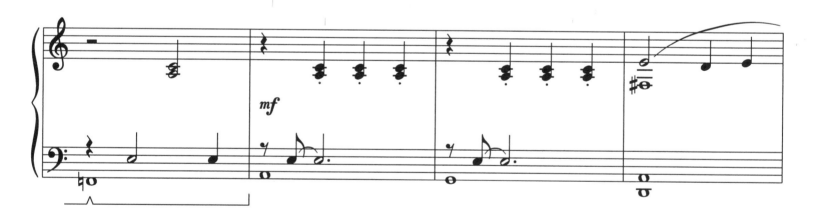

# LESSON: YESTERDAY

Beautiful in its simplicity, the Beatles' song "Yesterday" rates as one of the most popular songs of all time. Sparse textures and spare harmonies give this song its understated character. Let's take a look at one section of this harmony to see how it's put together.

The song starts in the key of F major, using an F major chord throughout the first three measures. In measure four the harmony takes a left turn and goes from an E minor seven chord, to an A seven followed by a D minor chord in bar five. The harmony here grabs our ear but somehow seems to make great sense as well. Let's take a closer look.

The overall goal in the first few measures of the verse (bars three to five) is to get from an F major chord to a D minor chord, two closely-related harmonies. The only difference between them is a single note, D.

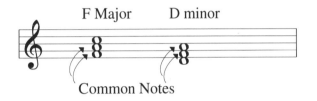

Instead of going directly from an F chord to the D minor, two other chords are inserted in between, an E minor seven and an A seven. These two chords are used as a transition to the D minor harmony. They lead to the D minor by a common progression of perfect fifths. The E minor chord is fifth above the A seven, while the A seven is a fifth above the D minor, our goal. Often chords that are a fifth above, or even two chords as in our case, are used to approach a goal chord. Look for this and other similar chord progressions whenever some specific harmony attracts your attention.

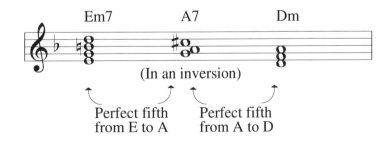

# YESTERDAY

Words and Music by
JOHN LENNON and PAUL McCARTNEY

**Moderately and expressively**

MCA music publishing

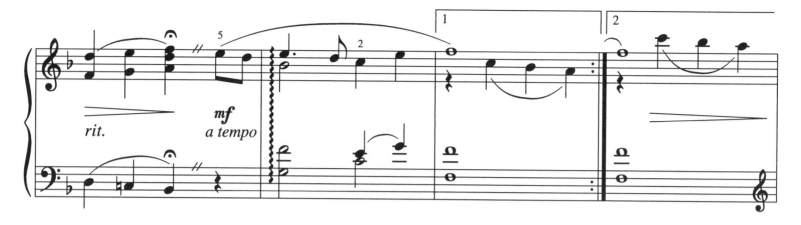

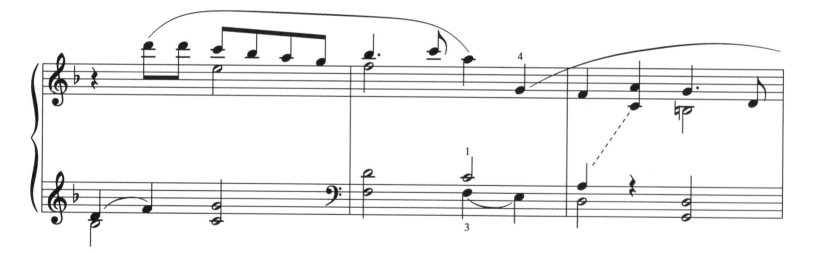

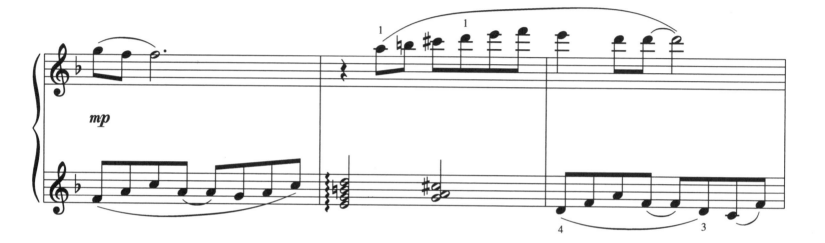